I0845813

Conquering New Heights

Virtual Reality and Mountaineering from Home

Table of Contents

Chapter 1. Introduction

Searching for new thrills and heights from the comfort of your home? Look no further than our latest Special Report, "Conquering New Heights: Virtual Reality and Mountaineering from Home." This document offers an exhilarating journey into the enthralling world of virtual reality (VR), an innovative technology that has revolutionized how we approach mountaineering and other high-adventure sports. Our investigation takes you from the ice-capped peaks of the Himalayas to the steep cliffs of Yosemite, all while remaining snug at your dwelling. With our guidance, you will learn how VR could change your life, whether you're a seasoned mountaineer seeking additional training tools or simply a home-bound adventurer longing for the thrill of the climb. Don't miss out on this fantastic voyage where technology meets the call of the wild. Get ready to conquer new heights...right from your living room!

Chapter 2. Exploring the Virtual Landscape: An Introduction

In an era increasingly dominated by digital technology, virtual reality (VR) has emerged as a cutting-edge tool shaking up diverse domains, from gaming and entertainment to healthcare and education. Indeed, many activities traditionally experienced in physical terms are now transcending into a virtual space, and mountaineering is one. Combining technology's prowess with our innate thrill for adventures, VR is promising a unique experience of climbing some of the world's most daunting peaks without ever stepping out of your home.

2.1. The Concept of Virtual Reality

Virtual Reality is an immersive simulator designed to mimic real-life experiences. Using a sophisticated combination of hardware and software, VR creates an artificial environment that not only looks real, but is interactive, engaging our senses in ways that conventional entertainment media can't. The technology's critical subset, computer graphics, works at achieving high fidelity in conjunction with a VR headset's stereoscopic display. Sensors track users' head and hand movements, translated into the VR world, making the simulated experience responsive and convincing.

Primarily, VR falls into two categories. The first, semi-immersive VR, provides a partial yet significant virtual experience as users are allowed to interact with a partially virtual environment using real-world elements. Flight simulators are an excellent example of this. The second category, fully immersive VR, delivers a comprehensive life-like experience by stimulating multiple senses simultaneously. This type is currently in high demand in the entertainment industry, from video gaming to virtual tours of tourist destinations, and now, in VR mountaineering.

2.2. Understanding VR Mountaineering

Virtual Mountaineering aims to recreate the daunting yet exhilarating adventure of mountain climbing. While it does not completely substitute the adrenaline rush one feels on an actual mountain, it permits users to learn techniques, understand challenges, and relish the scenery synonymous with such adventures. It's an exclusive blend of entertainment, skill learning, and safe exposure to health-related benefits of mountaineering.

The heart of VR Mountaineering is the simulation of dangerous, otherwise inaccessible environments that climbers aspire to conquer. High-end computer graphics render real-world landscapes and convert them into 360-degree images or videos. For large mountain ranges such as Mt. Everest or K2, this involves complex modeling techniques, satellite imagery, and multiple photos stitched together to simulate the mountain's real shape and texture. These images are further backed by sound simulations of whipping winds, avalanches, and animal sounds to recreate a fully immersive environment.

2.3. Hardware and Software Interface

At the heart of any VR system is the hardware interface that works in tandem with the software to immerify users. This typically includes a head-mounted display (HMD), handheld controllers, and often, body-tracking sensors.

HMDs are, de facto, the primary device used for experiencing VR. They incorporate screens for each eye, creating a stereoscopic effect, and are equipped with sensors to track head motion. These displays put users at the center of action, rendering a convincing depth of field. Most HMDs come with built-in headphones for a 3D positional sound experience.

Handheld controllers are crucial for navigation and interaction within VR. They may come in many shapes, with multiple buttons, triggers, and touchpad interfaces. Some high-end VR systems utilize gloves laden with sensors for a more tangible virtual experience.

Body-tracking sensors trace movements of the user's body within the physical space, which are mapped onto their virtual avatar. The sensors provide real-time tracking, enabling players to duck, dodge, or jump virtually.

The software plays an equally critical role. It translates the physical inputs into real-time actions within the VR world. It employs complex rendering algorithms and physics simulations to create an environment that responds to user inputs realistically. Developers integrate layers of interactivity, from object manipulation to moving routes, to make virtual climbing a compelling and rewarding challenge.

2.4. Climbing from the Comfort of Home

The beauty of VR Mountaineering is that it can be experienced from anywhere. This feature is especially appealing to those who may not have the physical potentials or resources to climb real mountains. It also serves as a training tool for prospective climbers, allowing them to practice scaling techniques, build muscle memory, and understand potential challenges without risking their lives.

However, beneath the thrill of conquering simulated peaks lies a potential health booster. Research suggests that VR experiences can have a range of positive psychological impacts, from reducing anxiety to enhancing mood, to providing a form of cognitive training.

2.5. A Word of Caution

While VR mountaineering holds immense potential and benefits, it's important to remember that it's a simulated experience. It should not substitute actual training and conditioning necessary for real-life mountaineering. Going up a real mountain involves much more than good climbing techniques. It requires physical fitness, mental resilience, and an understanding of natural forces one may face.

Also, the immersive nature of VR may trigger motion sickness in some users, known as cybersickness. This might include symptoms such as nausea, dizziness, and sometimes, a temporary impact on balance and coordination. Consequently, it's advised to take regular breaks and avoid prolonged exposure.

Ultimately, VR mountaineering opens up exciting new possibilities. It offers an unprecedented chance for users to experience, learn, and enjoy climbing, whether they're a seasoned mountaineer or a thrill-seeking home adventurer. In tandem with actual mountaineering, this transformative technology offers a gateway to new horizons, blending the thrill of the wild with the comfort of your home.

Chapter 3. Virtual Reality 101: Understanding the Tech Behind the Thrill

Before jumping into the world of embodied mountaineering experiences enabled by virtual reality, it's important to understand the remarkable technology that drives this thrill. So, we begin our journey by delving into some basics of VR, its historical context, the way VR systems work, and their applications beyond extreme sports.

VR technology isn't a new concept. In fact, we first saw the idea of a simulated, immersive environment brought to life as far back as the 1960s with the Sensorama machine developed by Morton Heilig. Since then, the concept and execution of VR have grown leaps and bounds with advancements in technology.

3.1. The Basics of VR

In essence, VR is a simulated experience that can be similar to or entirely different from the real world. It leverages sophisticated technology to create a convincing representation of an imaginary or real environment, allowing users to interact with this environment in a seemingly real way.

The goal of VR is to create a sensory experience that encompasses sight, touch, hearing, and occasionally even smell. For instance, with high-quality VR, you can look around a made-up environment as if you were truly present in the VR world, or use VR controllers to manipulate objects in the digital world just as in real life.

3.2. Components of VR

Typically, modern VR systems consist of two key elements:

1. A Head-Mounted Display (HMD): This device, worn on the user's head, presents 3D virtual images on screens placed very close to the eyes. There are different kinds of HMD, but they all essentially serve the same purpose: to work with your sight to create convincing immersive surroundings.

2. A Data Glove or Controllers: This element registers natural body movements and translates them into digital actions. When you move your hands in the real world, the corresponding action is detected and recreated in the virtual world to enhance immersion.

Some sophisticated VR systems also include full-body suits or treadmills to simulate physical movements, but these are not as commonly used and are mostly limited to specialized VR centers or professionals.

3.3. How Does VR Work?

There's a lot of science and technology behind the experience of VR. To deliver a visceral, real feeling, VR headsets need to respond to your head movements seamlessly. Known as 'six degrees of freedom (6DOF)', this movement covers forward/back, up/down, left/right, pitch, yaw, and roll.

The VR headset locates your position in the room and adjusts the images on your screen to reflect the perspective you would have in the real world. It uses two feeds sent to one display or two LCDs, one per eye, creating a stereoscopic effect with depth perception. This is the fundamental principle behind the 'gut-feeling' you get when you look down from a high mountain in a VR game.

3.4. VR Beyond Gaming

While VR's applications in gaming are well-known, its potential stretches far beyond that. In education, VR can provide interactive, immersive experiences that can significantly enhance learning. Meanwhile, industries such as real estate and tourism are using VR to provide virtual tours of properties and destinations.

In healthcare, professionals use VR for applications ranging from surgical training to therapy for PTSD. And of course, in sports and fitness, VR technologies provide users with an exciting, immersive way to engage in physical activities at home, with mountaineering being one of those activities.

3.5. The Future of VR

As technology continues to advance, so too will VR. We're seeing trends towards greater immersion and realism, more interactive experiences, and an increasing number of applications. In the realm of VR-enhanced sports training, there are glimpses of how breakthroughs in haptic technology will make simulated environments feel even more real.

With continued innovation in VR technology, the border between the simulated and the real will continue to blur. This holds the promise of even more thrilling and authentic mountaineering experiences in the comfort of your home, potentially transforming how we approach extreme sports and adventure.

In the following chapter, we will dive deeper into how VR technology shapes the experience of virtual mountaineering, making it more than just an exciting game, but a feasible training tool for both enthusiastic novices and seasoned professionals.

Chapter 4. VR Mountaineering: Evolution and Impact

In the early 1960s, the idea of immersing our senses in a virtual environment was no more than the stuff of science fiction. Fast-forward five decades, virtual reality (VR) has become a significant technological evolution capable of pushing the frontiers of human experience. A profound instance of its impact is on mountaineering, where, devoid of any actual risk, one can experience the thrills of scaling the world's highest peaks from the safety of their homes.

4.1. The Dawn of VR Mountaineering

The concept of VR mountaineering was born out of the necessity to provide mountaineers with a safe, low-cost, and easily accessible platform to hone their skills. With the proliferation of VR technology, developers began to create realistic experiences replicating some of the most challenging mountain terrains globally, changing traditional mountaineering forever.

The first primitive forms of VR mountaineering were shaky at best, with lackluster graphics and rudimentary controls. However, consistent efforts and advancements in VR and 3D rendering technologies led to the simulation of mountainous environments that gave users the sense of standing atop towering peaks, complete with icy winds and spectacular snowscapes.

4.2. Becoming Reality: Technological Innovations in VR

The integration of 360-degree cameras markedly improved VR mountaineering experiences. These cameras could capture every angle of a climbing expedition, which developers used to create simulations that gave users the sensation of making the arduous trek themselves. As the cameras became smaller and more sophisticated, climbers started equipping them on their expeditions, contributing to the growing repository of immersive VR mountaineering content.

Another crucial development was the introduction of VR treadmills. These machines mirrored the user's in-game movements, providing the physical exertion aspect missing in earlier models. Now, users had to physically strain themselves to climb these virtual mountains, making for a more immersive experience.

Simultaneously, haptic technology became vitally integrated into VR equipment. Haptic gloves allowed users to "feel" the rock surfaces and get a tactile sense of the thrill involved in actual mountaineering.

4.3. The Impact of VR on Professional Mountaineering

The advent of this technology had an immense impact on professional mountaineering. Training that previously required traveling to specific locations with suitable terrain could now occur anywhere with a VR setup, reducing both costs and logistical hindrances. Prospective climbers could acclimatize themselves to the vertiginous heights and austere conditions of famous peaks such as Everest, all within a controlled, risk-free environment. Moreover, it provided an excellent platform for climbers to mentally prepare, reducing the possibility of panic or disorientation during actual climbs.

Another significant advantage was the option to conquer particularly dangerous peaks virtually, previously deemed impossible due to perilous conditions. This feature enabled mountaineers to experience and understand some of the most challenging terrains, further pushing the boundaries of this sport.

4.4. Changing the Spectator Experience

VR Mountaineering also revolutionized how spectators engaged with the sport. As opposed to watching from the sidelines, fans could now become a part of the action. They could view the precipitous drops, feel the numbing cold, and experience the exhilaration of reaching the summit, all from the comfort of their homes.

Documentaries and films began harnessing the immersive power of VR, creating never-before-seen perspectives of mountaineering. This shift triggered a new wave of interest in the sport, exponentially expanding its audience.

4.5. The Future of VR Mountaineering

The potential of VR in mountaineering is vast and mostly untapped. As advancements continue, developers are aiming to create simulations so accurate they can be used as powerful training tools for professional climbers.

In the near future, we may see machine learning algorithms used in tandem with VR technology to tailor training regimens specifically for individual climbers, based on their strengths and weaknesses. These personalized programs could massively augment training effectiveness and safety within the sport.

In conclusion, the evolution and impact of VR on mountaineering have been transformative, heralding a new era in this high-intensity sport. These advancements have not only made mountaineering more accessible but have also freed it from its geographical constraints, allowing novice and seasoned climbers alike to conquer new heights on their terms. This exciting field continues to grow, and with developments on the horizon, VR mountaineering promises to scale even greater heights in the future.

Chapter 5. Advancements in VR Equipment: High Tech Meets High Altitude

Ascend with us as we navigate the technological landscapes of VR that are rapidly transforming high-altitude experiences and adventure sports. Once upon a time, mountaineering was perceived as an elite endeavor reserved for those with unwavering bravery and physical prowess. Today, however, thanks to advancements in VR technology, these peaks of travail and determination can be conquered by anyone – physically or virtually - irrespective of location or physical conditions.

5.1. Pioneering Brands in VR mountaineering

In the realm of VR technology, a multitude of brands are climbing to new heights and leading the pack in innovations that cater specifically to mountaineering enthusiasts. Brands such as Oculus, Sony, and HTC are cracking the code in providing highly immersive VR experiences for climbing.

Oculus, renowned for its Rift and Quest series, offers various mountaineering experiences with high-fidelity environments and seamless controls that mimic the physical realities of a grueling climb. Sony's PlayStation VR system also offers a plethora of immersive climbing experiences, with the added benefit of compatibility with the popular gaming console. HTC, on the other hand, is known for its Vive series which combines immersive room-scale VR with high-resolution displays for a truly realistic mountaineering experience.

5.2. Hardware Advances: VR Headsets

High-quality VR begins with a VR headset, the lynchpin for any immersive experience. The latest headsets offer improved field of view (FOV), higher resolution displays, and better refresh rates. FOV, which determines the extent of the observable environment at any given time, has become more expansive, paralleling natural human vision. The resolution of VR displays matches, if not outclasses, a human retina's experience in reality, often boasting 4K or higher capabilities, thus providing a crystal-clear depiction of the virtual world.

Enhanced refresh rates ensure that the virtual view adjusts swiftly and smoothly as you maneuver through the VR environment. This aids in reducing latency, which is vital for preventing motion sickness, a common detraction from the VR experience.

Another hardware advancement is the incorporation of eye-tracking technology. This feature supports dynamic foveated rendering – where the VR system focuses computational resources on where the eyes are looking, while reducing details in peripheral vision. This not only optimizes performance but also creates a more realistic visual experience.

5.3. The Rise of Haptic Feedback

As important as the visual journey are the tactile sensations that accompany a real climb. To replicate the feeling of gripping cold, hard rock or the vibrations from a crumbling ledge, haptic technology is rapidly integrating with VR equipment.

Gloves like the Manus VR and the Haptic Glove by Sensoryx incorporate sensors and tiny motors to stimulate the nerves in your hands, creating a sensation of touch and texture. Vest-like devices, such as the Teslasuit and the bHaptics Tactsuit, extend these sensations to the entire body. These vests produce stimuli that mimic environmental conditions, such as wind, enabling users to feel a chilling alpine breeze or the rough friction of a climbing rope.

5.4. Revolutionizing Soundscapes: 3D Audio

Another element vital to immersive VR experiences is sound — and 3D audio technology is making leaps and bounds in this arena. Spatial audio mimics the real-world behavior of sound, adding depth and directionality to auditory experiences. This means you can hear an eagle's cry overhead or the crunch of snow underfoot, distinguishing not just the type of sound but also the direction it came from, authentically simulating an outdoor environment.

5.5. Innovation in VR Software: Realistic Worlds to Explore

Delving into the software realm, tech producers are investing heavily in creating as lifelike an environment as possible. Photorealistic games and applications are available that simulate popular climbing spots down to their smallest details.

Applications such as Google's Tilt Brush allow users to design and navigate their own mountaineering tracks in 3D. The Everest VR application transports climbers to the infamous mountain, and The Climb – a critically acclaimed title by Crytek – offers a rich selection of climbing locations, each complete with their unique challenges.

5.6. VR Training and its Future

VR mountaineering goes beyond mere virtual tourism – it is also an effective training tool. It provides a risk-free arena where both amateur and seasoned mountaineers can practice climbing techniques and strategies, even simulating emergency scenarios, before attempting real-life ascents.

The future of VR equipment promises even more immersive and realistic experiences. With advancements such as the development of lightweight, wireless headsets, VR technology can only be expected to climb higher. The introduction of AI and machine learning could also lead to adaptive environments that respond to a user's skills and performance, providing personalized training and enhancing our climbing experiences.

In conclusion, VR technology's rapid advancements are transforming the landscape of mountaineering and making it accessible in unprecedented ways. The innovation journey mirrors the spirit of mountaineering, keeping us on our toes with constant suspense and anticipation as we scale towards future discoveries. Happy climbing!

Chapter 6. Safety in Simulated Heights: Real Precautions in a Virtual World

Even as we saunter into the arena of virtual reality mountaineering, safety considerations must come to the forefront. With giants strides in technological advancements like VR, we can enjoy tough mountainous terrains right from the comfort of our homes. Nonetheless, understanding the risks of a VR environment is critical to a safe and enjoyable experience. This section will illuminate the necessary precautions, offering a thorough safety guide for your virtual adventure.

6.1. Understanding VR: A New Terrain

The first step towards safe use of a virtual reality system is understanding what it entails. Virtual Reality, by its nature, creates an illusion, tricking our senses into believing we are somewhere we are not. It does this by presenting us with identical stimuli to what we would experience in that exact situation. Consequently, we respond as if we were in the simulated environment, while physically still in our homes.

Understanding this dual existence is the first step towards safety. While VR leads us into awe-inspiring heights, we must remember the actual setting remains stationary and often cramped. Awareness of your surroundings helps prevent bumping or tripping over furniture, stepping on pets, or running into walls, thus ensuring your experience is safe and untarnished.

6.2. Equipment Safety

Prior to embarking on your simulated mountaineering adventure, confirm that all your equipment is functioning correctly. Faulty equipment can cause accidents and injuries, aside from ruining the virtual climbing experience. Regular maintenance includes cleaning the gear properly after every use, storing in a dust-free environment, and periodically checking for any damage or flaws.

Headsets: The primary tool in your VR journey. Carefully monitor it for any cracks and always clean the lenses. Controllers: Another vital element. Regularly check for any irregularities like broken buttons or joystick issues that might hamper your navigation through the virtual world. Haptic Feedback Gloves and Suits: These add a physical dimension to your virtual experiences. Be sure they're free of hazards like electrical shorts or loose parts.

6.3. Environmental Setup

Equally crucial is the environment where you set up your VR gear. The more spacious, the better since you'll be moving around quite a bit – imagine trying to scale a vertical rock face. Clear any clutter or potential tripping hazards from your vicinity. Remember, once you have your headset on, you'll have limited visibility of the real world.

A good tip is to use the 'guardian system' that most VR setups offer. This feature enables you to outline a safe space in your room. If you approach beyond these boundaries, a warning signal will alert you, so you can return to the safer central area.

6.4. Physical Check-ups

Engaging in virtual mountaineering requires robust health. Even though you're not physically climbing a mountain, the physical exertion can be almost as intense. It's advisable to have regular check-ups to ensure you're fit for this activity.

In some VR mountaineering applications, there can be real-world implications such as motion sickness or even a form of vertigo. If you're susceptible to such conditions, it's essential to take extra precautions and perhaps look for different types of experiences that won't cause such discomfort.

6.5. Appropriate Segregation of Virtual and Real

Though virtual mountaineering gives you a fantastic experience of climbing mountains from your living room, it's crucial to remember that this is a simulation. The principles and techniques you learn in the VR world might not translate directly to real-life mountaineering. The weather, terrain inconsistencies and your physical stamina react differently in real life.

Never underestimate the vital aspect of safety gear and professional supervision in real-world mountaineering. VR should be treated as a supplementary tool for thrill, exercise, or learning basics rather than a substitute for the actual experience.

6.6. Mental Health Considerations

Lastly, though VR can bring us thrilling experiences, it can also potentially stress our mental health. Extended time in VR can lead to detachment, disorientation or feelings of isolation. Just like managing your physical health, it is critical to manage your mental wellbeing. Limit your time in VR, and ensure you maintain a balance with other aspects of your life.

In conclusion, the journey through virtual heights brings with it a unique array of safety considerations. As we embrace this novel way of experiencing the thrill of adventure, safety must always be our paramount concern. By adhering to these guidelines, you are set to explore soaring heights with the assurance of safety.

Remember, in the enthralling world of virtual reality mountaineering, the most important climb is the one that keeps you safe and thriving both off and on the virtual trail.

Chapter 7. Training and Conditioning: VR as a Doorway to Real Mountaineering

Mountaineering, traditionally, calls for a variety of skills and abilities such as endurance, strength, technical skill, and mental toughness. These skills are usually gained through physically demanding training, often coupled with lifestyle changes. But, how can you train for a high-altitude climb in the confines of your home? This is where Virtual Reality (VR) steps in, offering a potential breakthrough in mountaineering training and conditioning.

7.1. Emulating Real-life Adventures

One of the most significant advantages of VR training is its capability to replicate real-world scenarios more realistically and vividly than any traditional training methods. This technology can simulate climb conditions such as thin air at high altitudes, unstable footings, steep slopes, and harsh weather conditions, helping you anticipate and prepare for them without risking life and limb.

In addition, VR tech can mimic the unique physical demands of mountaineering. Ever wondered how your body might cope with the challenges of an expedition? VR tech can replicate the strain on your muscular and cardiovascular system, so you better understand the exertion levels of climbing, thereby learning to manage your energy more efficiently.

VR can also provide exposure to tricky techniques used in mountaineering such as self-arresting with an ice axe, tying knot systems, or rappelling, all within the safety of your own living environment.

7.2. Enhancing Mental Strength and Preparedness

Mountaineering is as much a mental challenge as it is a physical one. This is where VR shines as it creates realistic, immersive environments that challenge your mental strength and decision-making capability.

For example, it can replicate situations that present dilemmas like deciding whether to press on or retreat in the face of an unexpected storm, or choosing between different ascent routes. This mental exposure to situations that might be life-threatening in reality, prepare you mentally and emotionally for the tough calls you might have to make when you're actually climbing.

7.3. Physical Conditioning with VR

While real-life, outdoors physical conditioning is irreplaceable, VR training can significantly supplement it. Virtual reality systems integrated with treadmills, climbing walls, and resistance bands can simulate the unique exertion that mountaineering demands. For example, you might find yourself virtually climbing a steep rocky outcrop with a heavy backpack, all the while given the resistance and feel of doing the task in real conditions.

This type of VR training is not only safe but can be repeated as many times as you wish, allowing you to focus on building specific muscle groups, increasing your stamina, or working on your climbing technique—all crucial aspects of performance on real mountains.

7.4. Learning from the Experts

Tooling up with the latest VR tech offers a chance to learn from experienced mountaineers who might be thousands of miles away or from pre-recorded VR training sessions from renowned climbers. This revolutionary leap allows you to gain insights into the minds and practices of people who have conquered these challenging landscapes in reality.

7.5. Nurturing Safety Practices

Safety is paramount in mountaineering, and VR can help to instill good safety practices. You can rehearse emergency procedures and risk control measures until they become second nature, which in a real emergency could make the difference between life and death.

VR tech can simulate scenarios like getting caught in an avalanche or a crevasse fall, giving you the chance to practice emergency rescue actions in circumstances that could be deadly in the real world.

Virtual Reality is not just a convenience - it's a way of making your mountaineering safer, more efficient, and even more adventurous. Embracing this technology opens up a whole new dimension of possibilities from learning the ropes more rapidly to refining your mental strength, all while nestled at home. It presents opportunities to improve yourself mentally, technically, and physically, ensuring that when you finally make the climb for real, you are as prepared as it is possible to be.

In an era where technology has become a cornerstone of our daily lives, why not use this marvel to the best of our advantage. After all, being atop a mountain peak is not just about witnessing breathtaking views; it's about relishing the journey you undertook to reach there. And Virtual Reality can undoubtedly prepare you better for that extraordinary journey. So, conquer the mountains both virtually and in reality, and bask in the unprecedented experience!

Chapter 8. Immerse in Adventure: This is What a VR Climb Feels Like

Immerse in Adventure begins with an imaginative exploration of the ethereal experience of a VR climb, leading the reader gently from the mundane room-space into the boundless world of virtual reality.

The first step in embarking on any VR climb is strapping on your headset. As your VR device covers your forehead and eyes like a visored helmet, you're preparing to step into another realm. As you glimpse the 360-degree view, what was once your living room, kitchen, or garage fades away as your new digital surroundings take hold.

Beyond the headset, putting on the physical controllers is akin to strapping on your boots and picking up your ice axe, as these will serve as your limbs in the virtual world. Sensing the weight of the controllers in your hands and feeling the straps against your wrists, you begin to feel the anticipatory sensations of the climb to come.

8.1. The Virtual Becomes Real

In no time at all, you're standing at the foot of a towering, majestic mountain. You crane your neck upwards to glimpse the peak, far off in the clouded distance. The controllers in your hands now feel like sturdy carabiners, and you flex your fingers, hearing the metallic clang and feeling the vibration that mimics the motion perfectly.

As you begin your ascent, each inch of progress is a testament to the incredible precision of the VR experience. Every gripped ledge, every foot planted on a precarious outcrop delivers astounding hyper realism. You can almost feel the chilling wind whip past your face, hear the icy crumbles of snow underfoot. Every move you make is echoed in the lifelike physics of the digital terrain.

8.2. Scaling the Heights

As you continue climbing, finding purchase on crevices and ledges, making challenging leaps across yawning chasms, the immersion deepens. The sun moves steadily across the sky. Shadows grow longer as you scale the heights, and the temperature visibly drops around you. Even though you're comfortably at home, you can sense the chill of the glaciers and ridges.

Look down, and you'll see a sweeping vista of land and sky stretching out beneath you, landforms rolling and dipping in natural beauty. Look up, and the peak of the mountain quivers in your sight, an almost reachable goal.

8.3. The Final Push

You've scaled most of the mountain now. You look down and marvel at the amount you have climbed. Your heart races as your avatar takes deep, labored breaths. But the summit is close. You push on with renewed determination. The wind howls ominously, the narrow peak presents formidable challenges. All around, the steep drop-offs are a gripping reminder of the dizzying heights you have conquered.

A final scramble up a sheer cliff, a leap of faith across a narrow crevice, and you are victorious. You've reached the summit. Up here, the world stretche out beneath you in all its panoramic glory—an astonishingly realistic view rendered from databases of topographical and satellite imagery.

8.4. The Descent

The climb down is a different kind of journey, a meditation on the accomplishment of your recent feat. The descent provides its own adventurous challenges. Timing and precision are key as you rappel and slide down the risky slopes, all the while surrounded by the stunning vistas of your virtual environment.

What began as a simulation in your living room has become an adrenaline-thrill filled journey. The noises, the physics, the sights, all render a near-perfect illusion of reality that transcends typical gaming or simulation fare.

In your heart-pounding adventure, you've experienced something remarkable. Today, you scaled one of the world's greatest mountains. The thrill, the challenge, the sheer joy of it is indescribable. You remove the VR headset and the controllers, slowly returning to reality, your heartbeat still echoing the excitement of the climb.

Through this immersive journey, VR technology takes a timeless human adventure—the quest to scale the mountain, to reach new heights—and brings it within reach for everyone, everywhere. No matter where you are, be it your living room, bedroom or garage, the mountain is now only a VR headset away. The mountaintop, once a distant dream for many, can now be grasped in the palm of your hands.

And so, this is what a climb feels like. The thrill, the fear, the joy, and finally, the triumph. Tomorrow, who knows? Another mountain awaits. The thrill of orienteering in a Bulgarian forest, canyoning in the French Alps, or perhaps ice climbing in the crags of Scotland. The possibilities are as vast and as varied as the contours of the globe itself. Unleash your inner adventurer; discover, explore and conquer. The world is waiting, right in your living room.

Chapter 9. Peak Performance: Interviews with VR Mountaineering Enthusiasts

High-tech mountaineering is no longer confined to the realms of science fiction. With the advent of virtual reality (VR), climbing enthusiasts and professionals can experience the adrenaline rush of conquering mountain peaks from the comfort of their homes. In this chapter, we feature conversations with passionate VR mountaineering fans across skill and experience levels. Their insights illustrate the enormous potential of VR technology in revolutionizing mountaineering and outdoor adventure.

9.1. Embracing the Digital Wilderness: The Beginner's Perspective

Our journey commences with Sarah, a VR amateur who opted for digital mountaineering to overcome a lifelong fear of heights. With no prior experience in either climbing or VR, she found herself immersed in an environment that combined challenge with safety. "Despite standing in my living room, I was mentally scaling a crag with snow biting at my goggles," she recalls. Sarah's ascent of the digital Matterhorn was a milestone that transformed her concept of personal limits. "Without the physical barriers, I found my fear dissipating," she says, emphasizing the psychological empowerment that VR mountaineering can offer.

9.2. Scaling New Virtual Peaks: The Intermediate Climber's Take

Our next conversation is with James, an intermediate-level mountaineer who turned to VR during rehabilitation after a serious climbing injury. For James, VR simulators became a means to retain his skills and strength when physical exercise was impossible. James's experience raises the possibility of using VR as a viable training tool for mountaineers. "It is not a replacement for physical climbing, but a complementary tool that keeps your technique sharp," reflects James. He stresses that while VR cannot fully replicate the rigors of the sport, it plays an integral role in mental conditioning and technique refinement.

9.3. Beyond Real: Advanced Climbers and VR

At the pinnacle of VR mountaineering are the experts such as Amanda, a seasoned alpine explorer who has chalked up numerous real-world summits. A late convert to VR technology, she now embraces it as part of her training regimen, arguing that it offers a controlled environment to refine specific climbing techniques. According to Amanda, "There are situations you don't want to face unprepared on a real mountain. VR enables you to rehearse your response in a danger-free zone." She also values VR's ability to model distinct mountain environments, helping climbers anticipate challenges they may encounter.

9.4. Professional Climbers: Adopting VR in Training

Gaining insights from professional climbers like Mark, we find that

VR technology is well-accepted and potentially beneficial. Mark, a renowned mountaineer, uses VR for acclimation practice and to prepare himself for the distinct conditions specific to an upcoming climb. The realistic graphics and attention to detail in modern VR simulations provide an excellent platform to 'experience' different climbers' routes, estimate difficulty levels, and anticipate potential problems.

9.5. Climber's Haven: VR Developers on Creating Realistic Experience

The last segment of our exploration comprises an interaction with VR developers at InclineVR, a startup specializing in mountaineering VR simulations. Their team is collaborating with experienced climbers to recreate the accuracy of mountain landscapes, including specific routes up famous peaks. As part of its ambitious goals, the team aims to include simulating different weather conditions and altitudes. They believe in offering users the most realistic immersive experience possible, empowering climbers to train and hobbyists to explore without leaving home.

The rise of VR presents a tantalizing future for mountaineering that is not bound by geographical limitations, exceptional costs, or even physical readiness. As the technology evolves and simulation fidelity increases, the gap between real and virtual climbing may reduce further – opening a world of opportunities for both novices and seasoned climbers.

Thus, from conquering personal fears as Sarah did, to maintaining practice during injury recovery like James, or preparing for a challenging climb as in Amanda's and Mark's case, virtual mountaineering offers something for everyone. The intersection of VR and mountaineering seems to mark a new route to the peak—one offering unwavering thrills, undeterred by reality's constraints.

Chapter 10. Climbing Today, Tomorrow, and Beyond: The Future of VR Mountaineering

Mountaineering, in its traditional sense, is an activity that has long been defined by unadulterated human effort, an adventurous spirit, and a deep respect for nature's overwhelming forces. However, in the face of technological disruptions, this high-risk sport finds itself on the cusp of a new era. Intersections between technology and athleticism are not new, but the advent of Virtual Reality (VR) takes it to exceptional heights.

10.1. The Interface Between VR and Mountaineering

VR technology brings to users an immersive, three-dimensional experience that unhinges the imposed restrictions of physicality. VR in mountaineering is becoming an increasingly palpable reality made possible by the intricate web of interactive technologies. Users can virtually scale the treacherous cliffs of K2 or traverse the snow-laden slopes of Mont Blanc. These experiences are not limited to simple visual fare, but also involve tactile feedback, simulating conditions climbers would encounter in the actual scenario, such as gloved interaction with ice axes or carabiners.

10.2. How Current VR Technologies Shape Mountaineering

Current iterations of VR technology often use stereoscopic headsets with motion-tracking capabilities, and handheld devices to simulate the climbing experience. For instance, Crytek's "The Climb" lets players ascend without restraints, showering them with breathtaking vistas while doing so. It changes the way we understand sports, bringing the thrill right into our homes and letting us experience it as we would in person. Even professional climbers can use these technologies as training tools to get acquainted with treacherous routes they plan to ascend.

Simulators like MORIS (Mobile Rescue Simulator) can provide more realistic and life-like experiences for climbers undergoing training. They offer tailored scenarios of mishaps that can occur during a climb, preparing climbers for possible emergencies. But these technologies are just stepping stones to the future possibilities VR offers to mountaineering.

10.3. The Future of VR Mountaineering

Looking ahead, the role of VR in mountaineering extends beyond simple simulation. Integrated with biometric devices, future VR technologies could track climbers' vital signs, allowing them to understand their body's physical responses to different altitudes, temperatures, or exertions.

Moreover, using machine learning algorithms and experiential data, VR systems could be customized to match the climber's conditioning level or provide layered experiences to novice climbers looking to learn the ropes. Allied with AI, VR technologies could deliberate the climber's experience, analyzing actions, and suggesting improved climbing approaches.

Augmented Reality (AR), a close cousin of VR, also holds promise. AR overlays digital data onto the real world, a concept deployed in industries from education to surgery. In mountaineering, it could serve to navigate routes and provide pertinent information about the site's history, topology, local flora, and fauna, or record altitude, speed, and weather conditions.

10.4. Challenges and Considerations

However, VR technology's integration into mountaineering is not without hurdles. With the simulation of a risk-laden sport like mountaineering, there is a thin line between virtual and reality. Climbing requires a balance of physical and mental preparedness, and VR should not foster a false sense of prowess that could prove dangerous in real-life scenarios.

Moreover, the technological aspect of VR remains a privilege. Harnessing VR for climbers across geographic and economic strata is vital to a universally accessible future of mountaineering.

10.5. The Climber's Crucible: Physical to Virtual

Traditional mountaineering purists might argue that VR takes away the element of "authentic" adventure. However, VR represents the fusion of physicality with digital advancement, not its overthrow. The thrill of ascent, combined with next-generation technology, might just be the frontier of a new mountaineering culture, a blend of adrenaline and electrons. VR does not replace existing mountaineering practice; it supplements and evolves it.

In conclusion, the future of VR in mountaineering looks promising. With advancements in computing power, AI, and sensory hardware, VR will continue to revolutionize our understanding and approach towards mountaineering. The intersection of climber and coder, of peak and pixel, is an exciting new world to explore. Through VR, we can reach out to those colossal pinnacles we dream of - all from the comfort of home.

Chapter 11. A Climber's Guide: Selecting Your VR Mountaineering Equipment

Choosing the right equipment is crucial for a satisfying and immersive VR mountaineering experience. Be it the VR headset, controllers, or complementing accessories, your selection could significantly impact your virtual mountaineering journey.

11.1. VR Headset Selection

The VR headset is the core of your virtual reality gear. Fit, comfort, and visual quality are vital factors in your immersive experience.

11.1.1. Oculus Quest 2

The Oculus Quest 2 is an excellent choice for a few reasons. First, it is standalone, meaning that it does not require a PC or other peripheral devices to operate. Its lightweight, compact design and the addition of a head strap help with maintaining comfort during extended use. The device offers a resolution of 1832 x 1920 per eye, making it one of the best in its category.

11.1.2. HTC Vive Pro 2

The HTC Vive Pro 2 is designed for PC VR applications, offering a significant upgrade in terms of visual quality with a resolution of 2448 x 2448 pixels per eye. Moreover, its 120Hz refresh rate makes it easier for users to play for extended periods without experiencing nausea. The room-scale VR experience is one of its notable features.

11.1.3. Valve Index

Valve Index highlights "finger tracking," meaning the controllers can detect individual finger movements. This feature makes for immensely interactive gameplay. With a resolution of 1440 x 1600 pixels per eye, it offers quality visuals, while the 120Hz refresh rate negates motion sickness.

11.2. Choosing the Right Controllers

Controllers are an essential component of VR, allowing you to interact with the virtual world. Here are some options to consider.

11.2.1. Oculus Touch Controllers

Oculus Touch Controllers are designed for use with the Oculus Quest 2 headset. These controllers track your hand movements accurately. They also provide a variety of buttons for optimal control during games or simulations.

11.2.2. Valve Index Controllers

Known as 'Knuckles,' these controllers stand out due to their exceptional finger-tracking technology. These controllers fit comfortably and securely around your hand, offering an immersive experience where you can use your hands naturally.

11.2.3. HTC Vive Controllers

These controllers offer players plenty of options for control, a touchpad, trigger, and grip buttons. Compatible with HTC Vive headsets, the controllers enable a tactile gameplay experience.

11.3. Importance of Accessories

To enhance your overall VR mountaineering experience, consider adding a few accessories to your setup.

11.3.1. VR Cover

Comfort is significant in VR, and a VR cover provides an additional layer of comfort. It also helps in keeping the headset clean.

11.3.2. Prescription Lenses

If you wear glasses, prescription lenses could prove invaluable. They reduce the discomfort of having to wear glasses underneath the headset and eliminate the risk of scratching the headset lenses.

11.3.3. High-Quality Headphones

The sound is a crucial part of the immersive VR experience. The right pair of headphones can significantly enhance your overall experience, just be sure they're comfortable and have top-notch sound quality.

11.4. Understanding the Software

Software forms a significant part of the VR experience. A couple of noteworthy options include Everest VR and The Climb 2.

11.4.1. Everest VR

With Everest VR's awe-inspiring graphics and immersive experience, users can climb the summit of Mount Everest. The narrative experience is engaging and recreates the thrill of mountaineering.

11.4.2. The Climb 2

This software puts users right in the middle of breathtaking scenery. The user can choose different mountains to climb, increasing or decreasing the difficulty based on their preference.

Remember, gear alone won't instantly make you a great virtual mountaineer. Regardless of the equipment you choose, it's the time, dedication, and effort you put into learning and understanding the VR environment that genuinely makes the difference. Here's to conquering the highest peaks from the comfort of your home!

www.ingramcontent.com/pod-product-compliance
Lightning Source LLC
Chambersburg PA
CBHW060856260726
48661CB00008B/3304